Unless otherwise indi
quotations in this volume
Transla

©2016 Sherry Poundstone
FOCUS International
A Teaching Ministry for Women
Bethesda Reno-Tahoe
ISBN-10:1523994827

Requests for information should be directed to
FOCUS International
info@focuswomen.org
www.focuswomen.org
775-657-8413

All rights reserved. No part of this publication may be reproduced, stored in a retrieval system, or transmitted in any form or by any means-for example, electronic, photocopy, or recording-without the prior written permission of the publisher. The only exception is a brief quotation in printed reviews.

For the Kingdom of God is not just a lot of talk; it is living by God's power. 1 Corinthians 4:20

Becoming a Woman of Power with God

Freedom Series
Volume 2

Sherry Poundstone

Thank You

….to God for placing in me a desire to teach His word.

….to my husband, John, who believes I can do anything.

….to my dear friend, Diane, for reading and re-reading this study.

….to the FOCUS leadership team for their prayers.

What People Are Saying

"Sherry Poundstone is a gifted Bible study writer, and with her latest book *Becoming a Woman of Power with God* she's done it again! It's clear, concise, and anointed. I believe this Bible study will take women deep into God's Word and deep into His Presence, igniting a desire to walk in His power in fullness."
Paula Friedrichsen
Speaker and author of *A Season of Breakthrough*

"What a wonderful and engaging Bible Study! *Becoming a Woman of Power with God* speaks to the hearts of all women, from the baby Christian to the well-seasoned believer. Sherry Poundstone offers amazing insight and relevant scripture which so beautifully illustrates how our everyday situations can and will change when we simply plug into the power of our living, loving God. Not only does the reader learn more about the scriptures, but we learn more about ourselves, as she uses practical application to take us through the journey of becoming the women God intended us to be."
Debbie Dillon
Editor at *Christian Women's Voice Magazine*

"A woman fully submitted to Christ is a beautiful, powerful tool in the hands of God. The art of balancing poise with power is not easy to master, but is clearly taught in this book as Sherry weaves analogies with Scripture to help us find that position of power so precious from God's perspective."
Marnie Swedberg
International Leadership Mentor

"Sherry Poundstone has done a wonderful job presenting the Godly principle of becoming a woman of power. She offers practical advice alongside helpful tips in each chapter to help the reader apply the lesson. The text is grounded in scripture, but Sherry keeps a conversational tone that makes it easy to understand. *Becoming a Woman of Power with God* is a book that will take the Christian woman to the next level in her walk with God."
Nan Jones
Speaker and author of *The Perils of a Pastor's Wife*

Becoming a Woman of Power with God
Table of Contents

Welcome

Join Our Group

Prepare to Study

Lesson 1 - The Power of Power

Lesson 2 - Plug into God's Power

Lesson 3 - Timing is Everything-*Esther*

Lesson 4 - The Power of God's Guidance-*Ruth*

Lesson 5 - The Power of Prayer-*Hannah*

Lesson 6 - The Power of Humility-*Abigail*

Lesson 7 - The Power of Wisdom-*Deborah*

Lesson 8 - The Power of Devotion-*Priscilla*

Lesson 9 - The Power of Faith-*Sarah*

Lesson 10 - The Power of Inheritance-*Lois and Eunice*

Leader's Guide/Answer Key

Welcome to *Becoming a Woman of Power with God* Bible Study!

Whether you have been following Christ for many years or just a few days, I believe that this study on power will be of benefit to you. This 10 week study is designed for the individual or small group.

The suggested format for this study is to read through the lesson and scriptures completely, and then re-read for more insight. Complete the *Live it Out, Prayer Point, and Further Study* sections. Read the suggested chapter and verses in the *Moving On* portion in order to prepare for the next lesson.

Allow yourself plenty of time to really dig in and meditate on each of the scriptures listed with each lesson. If you need to come back to this section at another time, be sure to make an appointment with yourself to do just that.

When we commit a verse to memory, it will be there for us to pull on when needed. I suggest choosing one verse out of each list to memorize.

Blessings to you on your journey to *Becoming a Woman of Power with God.*

Sherry Poundstone

Join the FOCUS Study Group

Now you can join in with women from all over the world as you study *Becoming a Woman of Power with God*!

The online FOCUS study group was created to connect you with other women who are reading *Becoming a Woman of Power with God* and serves as a platform for discussion, comments or questions.

To become a part of our online group, please visit our *FOCUS International Study Groups* page on Facebook and request to join, or email **info@focuswomen.org**.

All proceeds from the sale of this book go to support the mission of FOCUS International-A Ministry for Women. **www.focuswomen.org**

Prepare to Study

1. Purposely set aside time. Make an appointment to study *Becoming a Woman of Power with God*. If you are in a small group, that will be the day and time you gather with other women. If you are working through this study on your own, try to set the same day and time for your study each week. Consistency is the key.

2. Prepare to study. Select a place or a room in your house where you can be alone. Somewhere you are comfortable and at peace. This may require some creativity if you are the mom of small children or have an active household. Perhaps a local coffee place or a park might work well for you. Design it to fit your life.

3. Have all your materials available. Consider creating a *Prayer Basket* to hold the materials you will need to study. Gather your Bible, *Becoming a Woman of Power with God* book, a journal/notebook, pens and highlighters in a nice basket or container. Having everything in one place will save you time and make it easier to begin. Access to a Bible dictionary or concordance will be helpful. There are many online options. One of my favorites is www.biblegateway.com

4. Prepare your heart. Talk to God about things you may need to confess, and enter your study time peacefully and without anything that may block you from receiving revelation during your study.

For God has not given us a spirit of fear and timidity, but of power, love, and self-discipline.
2 Timothy 1:7

Lesson 1

The Power of Power

For God has not given us a spirit of fear and timidity, but of power, love, and self-discipline.
2 Timothy 1:7

Webster's dictionary defines power as "the capacity or ability to *direct* or *influence* the behavior of others or the course of events."

Power is desired and pursued by individuals, countries, organizations and even church leaders. Power in itself is not a bad thing. The problem comes when it is used to control, abuse or destroy.

The desire for power can be motivated by a need to control or force our ideas and beliefs onto another person. Power can certainly be used in a negative and destructive way. On the other hand, if used correctly, power can positively influence people and change lives for the better. Power can create positive change in our personal lives, families, faith communities and cities.

Becoming a woman of power does not mean becoming a woman who controls and dominates. It does mean becoming a woman who influences her marriage, home, family, workplace, and faith community in a positive and edifying way. A woman of power builds up rather than tearing down.

When thinking of natural (worldly) power, we might picture in our minds physical strength and over-developed muscles. Today's popular super hero is a perfect example. Their power is used to save the good guys and destroy the enemy through brute force or super advanced technology.

Or, we may think of electrical power. We can all appreciate the luxury of plugging in an appliance to an electrical outlet, thus being able to cook, heat our home or blow dry our hair. In our culture, this type of power is taken for granted. Oh, the stress of a power outage as we are getting ready for work or preparing dinner!

Some years ago, I lived in a rural area where the electricity went out on a regular basis. One day, as happened so often, I was preparing for work when suddenly I had no electricity. It was very early in the morning, so it was dark in the house. I pulled my business suit and heels out of my closet in the dark and got dressed. Several hours later, I stood in front of a group of businessmen giving a presentation. I happened to look down and saw that I was wearing one black shoe and one blue shoe! The embarrassment as I realized that the men in the meeting had noticed. I certainly missed my electrical power that day.

God's power…..

For the Kingdom of God is not just a lot of talk; it is living by God's power. 1 Corinthians 4:20

God's power is amazing and wonderful. His power is not a controlling power but one of freedom and release. The supernatural power of God is immense and overwhelming. This is the power we must pursue as women of God. Not physical power but the supernatural power of God in submission to our Lord and Savior, Jesus Christ.

Jesus looked at them intently and said, "Humanly speaking, it is impossible. But with God everything is possible." Matthew 19:26

As we pursue this study of Becoming *a Woman of Power with God*, we will focus on growing into the power of God. We will study women of power in the Bible, and work toward allowing His power to guide our lives.

Live It Out

1. What is the difference between natural (worldly) power and the supernatural power of God?

2. God's power is one of freedom and release. What does that look like in our daily lives?

3. Matthew 19:26--*Jesus looked at them intently and said, "Humanly speaking, it is impossible. But with God everything is possible."* How easy or difficult is it for you to believe this verse? Give an example that these words are true from your own life.

Prayer Point

Write out a prayer praising God for His power in your life. Ask Him to show you specific examples. Ask Him to reveal any area of your life where you may be operating in your own power.

Further Study

Psalm 62:11
God has spoken plainly, and I have heard it many times: Power, O God, belongs to you...

_____ belongs to God.

1 Corinthians 6:14

And God will raise us from the dead by his power, just as he raised our Lord from the dead.

The same power that raised Jesus from the dead will _____.

Luke 11:20

But if I am casting out demons by the power of God, then the Kingdom of God has arrived among you.

The power of God can cast out _____.

Read the following scriptures and write out the key words and meaning of these verses.

2 Corinthians 13:4

Psalm 136:12

Job 9:4

Isaiah 26:4

Ephesians 6:10

Zephaniah 3:17

2 Corinthians 6:7

Job 26:14

Psalm 79:11

Pearls of Wisdom/Notes

Moving On

In preparation for Lesson 2, read 1 Chronicles 29:11 and Colossians 1:16.

Yours, O LORD, is the greatness and the power and the glory and the victory and the majesty, for all that is in the heavens and in the earth is yours. Yours is the kingdom, O LORD, and you are exalted as head above all.
1 Chronicles 29:11

Lesson 2

Plug in to God's Power

Yours, O LORD, is the greatness and the power and the glory and the victory and the majesty, for all that is in the heavens and in the earth is yours. Yours is the kingdom, O LORD, and you are exalted as head above all.
1 Chronicles 29:11

If we are to become women of power with God we must examine how to plug in to His power. God's power can show up in many ways! He provides the power source, but what is our part to play?

To begin with, we must humble ourselves before the Lord and submit our lives to Him. We must bow down to His greatness. We must acknowledge who He is in comparison to who we are and that He is all powerful. When we are humble before Him, God will lift us up. James 4:10 says *"Humble yourselves before the Lord, and he will lift you up in honor."* It's His power that will lift us up in honor. Humbling ourselves before the Lord enables us to submit to God. Submission is releasing control of our lives to Him. This does not mean that we have no responsibility or part to play in how we live. It does mean that we submit everything to Him and follow His lead and direction.

Submission to God is one of the main ways we can plug in to His power. Consider John 3:30 which says *"He must become greater and greater, and I must become less and less."* Living with God's power is allowing more of Him and less of us.

Let's look at some practical ways to plug into God's power.

Prayer…..
Prayer is communication with our Heavenly Father. It can be simple and uncomplicated conversation, and yet it is the fastest path to plugging into His power. Prayer is a two-way communication though. We must listen as well as speak!

Hearing and really listening to what the Lord has to say is just as important as placing all of our requests before Him. God doesn't work the same way all the time, and we need to hear His direction for each situation.

Your own ears will hear him. Right behind you a voice will say, "This is the way you should go," whether to the right or to the left. Isaiah 30:21

Keep on asking, and you will receive what you ask for. Keep on seeking, and you will find. Keep on knocking, and the door will be opened to you. Matthew 7:7

Seeking God's Presence…..
If we are motivated to plug into God's power, then we must create an atmosphere open to Holy Spirit and seek His presence.

Creating an atmosphere to host the Lord's presence will involve prayer, meditation on the Word, and worship. Each of us should develop what works for us. You may want to designate a certain room, or area of your home, to get quiet and seek His presence. Or perhaps there is a place in nature that makes it easy for you to seek God. There might be worship music that sets the stage. Each of us must do what works for us in seeking the Lord's presence.

Search for the LORD and for his strength; continually seek him. Psalm 105:4

Increased Faith…..
Increased faith enables us to plug into the power of God in a mighty way. The more faith we have the more of God's power we can tap into. The more powerful we become, the more we can accomplish what God is calling us to do.

Many years ago, during a very difficult time, I heard the words "crawl inside your Bible." I knew that the way to freedom was to get into the Word of God and stay there! I began reading and studying the Bible daily. My faith increased and peace enveloped me as a result.

So then faith comes by hearing, and hearing by the word of God. Romans 10:17 (NKJV)

As we pursue God's power, we may encounter interference. What kinds of things can get in the way of accessing the power God?

Let's look at some things that can get in our way of plugging into God's power.

Fear….. can paralyze our faith, our prayer life and keep us from plugging into God's power.
Fear never comes from God. In 2 Timothy 1:7 the word tells us *"For God has not given us a spirit of fear and timidity, but of power, love, and self-discipline."* Fear never comes from God and it can wreak havoc in our lives. God gave us power! In order to plug in, we must first recognize if we are living in fear. Pray and ask the Lord to show you the source. Pray and study the Word until you have victory over fear.

Unbelief….. can block us from plugging into God's power. I know that we would all like to say that we believe at all times, without doubt. But the truth is, we are all susceptible to unbelieving thoughts and actions. In the book of Mark, we read the account of the father of a demonized boy. *The father instantly cried out, "I do believe, but help me overcome my unbelief!"* Mark 9:24

The father in this situation believed for healing and deliverance of his son, and, at the same time, asked for help with his unbelief. It is easy to fall into this pattern of wrong thinking.

For example, I recently counseled a woman in the middle of a financial crisis. She is a strong believer in God and His power. However, worry and anxiousness had overtaken her. She was physically sick with worry. Once we prayed together for increased faith, and asked God to take the doubting thoughts away, she was at peace. Her situation had not changed, but by plugging into God's power, the unbelief was lifted.

Matthew 6:33 from The Message says it this way:
"…..Steep your life in God-reality, God-initiative, God-provisions. Don't worry about missing out. You'll find all your everyday human concerns will be met."

Learning to hear God's voice…..
My sheep listen to my voice; I know them, and they follow me. John 10:27

For us to plug into the power of God, we must learn to hear His voice. Learning to hear God's voice is invaluable. It is so easy for us to talk to God about what we need or want. But how much of our time with God is spent listening to His voice? The Lord constantly speaks to us and gives us His direction. We know from the word that He is always speaking.

Have you ever been driving down the street, been making dinner or working at your desk, when suddenly a thought comes to you out of nowhere? Maybe it's a solution to a problem or a great idea. Or perhaps you think of someone you haven't thought about in a while. Often, when an idea or thought comes to us in this manner, it is the Holy Spirit. This is God speaking to us. It doesn't have to be a booming, audible voice. We can practice hearing him.

Your own ears will hear him. Right behind you a voice will say, "This is the way you should go," whether to the right or to the left. Isaiah 30:21

How can we practice listening? Here are a few suggestions:

*Remove inner noise……*We must quiet the chatter in our minds. Often, thoughts of chores and tasks will create distraction. Keep a pad of paper handy to jot those down and put them out of your immediate thoughts. Some people find that softly playing background worship music helps.

*Remove outer noise…..*Pick a quiet room or an area of the house where there is less noise distraction. Perhaps a time of day when no one else is home, after everyone has gone to bed or before others get up in the morning. Whatever works best.

Get physically comfortable and calm….. Being uncomfortable can be a distraction. Choose a comfortable place to sit.

Pray, confess and repent….. then listen. Keep a journal, Bible and pen handy. Begin to write down the things that come to mind. Don't edit, just write.

Live It Out

1. List 3 ways we can plug into God's power.

2. How can you incorporate these into your daily life?

3. Fear and unbelief can cause interference when we are trying to plug into God's power. How? List some specific examples.

4. *Your own ears will hear him. Right behind you a voice will say, "This is the way you should go," whether to the right or to the left.* Isaiah 30:21
Think of a time when God spoke to you about a decision, choice or direction you should take.

Prayer Point

Write out a prayer praising God for His power in your life. Ask Him to reveal any areas of interference. Practice listening, and write down what you hear.

Further Study

Matthew 7:7
Keep on asking, and you will receive what you ask for. Keep on seeking, and you will find. Keep on knocking, and the door will be opened to you.

Jesus tells us to _____, _____ and _____ and He will give us what we need.

Matthew 21:22
You can pray for anything, and if you have faith, you will receive it.

If we have _____, we will _____.

Hebrews 11:1
Faith shows the reality of what we hope for; it is the evidence of things we cannot see.
Faith is what we _____ ___ but cannot ____.

Read the following scriptures and write out the key words and meaning of these verses.

Mark 11:24

John 14:13-14

Ephesians 3: 16-17

Mark 11:24

James 1:6

Hebrews 11:6

Romans 10:17

Isaiah 30:21

Hebrews 4:12

Pearls of Wisdom/Notes

Moving On

In preparation for Lesson 3, read through the book of Esther. Note the events and the power of God throughout the book.

✝

If you keep quiet at a time like this, deliverance and relief for the Jews will arise from some other place, but you and your relatives will die. Who knows if perhaps you were made queen for just such a time as this?
Esther 4:14

Lesson 3

Timing Is Everything
Esther

If you keep quiet at a time like this, deliverance and relief for the Jews will arise from some other place, but you and your relatives will die. Who knows if perhaps you were made queen for just such a time as this? Esther 4:14

God's power will show up in His perfect timing!

God's name is not mentioned in the Hebrew text of Esther, but He makes himself known in many ways. His presence and power fills the pages.

The book of Esther is an example of God's power and divine guidance over our lives. Throughout this book, we see an example of a woman of power. Esther's power source was God, and her courage and bravery was a direct result. The purpose of Esther's life events were to demonstrate God's sovereignty (supreme power and authority) and love for his people.

We can summarize the book of Esther with these highlights:
Esther becomes queen (1:1 – 2:23)
The Jewish people are threatened (3:1 – 4:17)
Esther intercedes for her people (5:1 – 8:17)
The Jewish people are delivered (9:1 – 10:3)

Esther is an account of circumstances that were essential to the survival of God's people in Persia. All of these events were God's design, proving that His power is sovereign over every area of life. We can take courage by allowing God to be in charge. His power can be our power. We may question certain situations or circumstances in our lives, but by drawing on the power of God we can make it through anything. Becoming a woman of power is putting our trust in God and having faith, no matter what the situation.

God gives us our position and power, to glorify and build His kingdom. Timing is everything. Esther was called on to intercede for and to save her people at a specific time. The Message Bible says it this way: *When Hathach told Mordecai what Esther had said, Mordecai sent her this message: "Don't think that just because you live in the king's house you're the one Jew who will get out of this alive. If you persist in staying silent at a time like this, help and deliverance will arrive for the Jews from someplace else; but you and your family will be wiped out. Who knows? Maybe you were made queen for just such a time as this.* Esther 4:12-14

God's power is displayed in His perfect timing. For us, that often means waiting longer than we like. Waiting can be difficult, but it is well worth it when we allow God to lead.

Over the years, God has blessed me with amazing opportunities and I have learned to wait on His timing. As a strong woman, I certainly have the capability to launch a project in my own timing, but, if I wait on God, His power will be behind my efforts. The results are worth waiting for.

God is calling us to be women of His power, and to use that power to influence our families, homes, workplaces and our nation.

Live It Out

1. What is the general theme of the book of Esther?

2. What were some of Esther's strengths and accomplishments?

3. How did God's power manifest in Esther's life?

4. Give an example of God's power and provision in your life. How important was the timing of the event or circumstance?

Prayer Point

Write out a prayer asking God to reveal an event in your life that displayed His perfect timing and power.

Further Study

Habakkuk 2:3
This vision is for a future time. It describes the end, and it will be fulfilled. If it seems slow in coming, wait patiently, for it will surely take place. It will not be delayed.

We are to _____ _____ for God's timing is perfect.

Isaiah 40:31
*But those who trust in the L*ORD *will find new strength. They will soar high on wings like eagles. They will run and not grow weary. They will walk and not faint.*

If we trust in the Lord, we will find ___ _____.

Galatians 6:9
So let's not get tired of doing what is good. At just the right time we will reap a harvest of blessing if we don't give up.

We will reap a harvest at the _____ _____.

Read the following scriptures and write out the key words and meaning of these verses.

Psalm 27:14

Ecclesiastes 8:6

Ecclesiastes 3:1

Proverbs 3:5-6

2 Peter 3:8

Psalm 37:3-4

Luke 18:27

Ecclesiastes 3:11

Lamentations 3:25-26

Pearls of Wisdom/Notes

Moving On

In preparation for Lesson 4, read through the book of Ruth. Note the general theme of her story.

✟

*But Ruth replied, "Don't ask me to leave you and turn back. Wherever you go, I will go; wherever you live, I will live. Your people will be my people, and your God will be my God. Wherever you die, I will die, and there I will be buried. May the L*ORD *punish me severely if I allow anything but death to separate us!"* Ruth 1:16-17

Lesson 4

The Power of God's Guidance
Ruth

> *But Ruth replied, "Don't ask me to leave you and turn back. Wherever you go, I will go; wherever you live, I will live. Your people will be my people, and your God will be my God. Wherever you die, I will die, and there I will be buried. May the LORD punish me severely if I allow anything but death to separate us!"* Ruth 1:16-17

God's power will show up through His guidance!

The book of Ruth shows the power of God and His guidance in Ruth's life. Let's look at a brief summary of Ruth's story.

Ruth was a Moabite woman and Naomi's daughter-in-law. Both Naomi and Ruth lost their husbands in Moab. There was almost nothing worse than being a widow at this point in history. Widows were usually poverty stricken, and often taken advantage of or ignored. Naomi found herself in a desperate situation. She decided to return to Israel, but encouraged her two daughters-in-law (Ruth and Orpah) to stay in Moab and make a fresh start. Orpah chose to stay in Moab. Ruth gave up the possibility of security and chose to follow and care for Naomi.

So Naomi returned from Moab, accompanied by her daughter-in-law Ruth, the young Moabite woman. They arrived in Bethlehem in late spring, at the beginning of the barley harvest. Ruth 1:22

Ruth decided to go into the fields at harvest time to gather heads of grain that had been dropped by the men harvesting. She chose a field to work that belonged to a wealthy relative of Naomi's husband. Boaz, the owner of this field, noticed her working and asked his foreman who she was. He was told that she was Ruth, Naomi's daughter-in-law.

This started an interesting sequence of events for Ruth. Boaz told her to work only his fields, he instructed his men to protect her and favor her with extra grain. He even asked her to eat and drink with his workers.

Boaz went over and said to Ruth, "Listen, my daughter. Stay right here with us when you gather grain; don't go to any other fields. Stay right behind the young women working in my field. See which part of the field they are harvesting, and then follow them. I have warned the young men not to treat you roughly. And when you are thirsty, help yourself to the water they have drawn from the well." Ruth 2:8-9

Ruth was prompted to go to a certain field not knowing that he was a relative that was able to take care of her and Naomi.

God guided her to this field because He had plans to bless Naomi and Ruth in ways far beyond their expectations. Boaz was a kinsman redeemer* of Naomi's husband and paid off their property and eventually married Ruth. Years later Jesus was born into this family line.

God's guidance in our lives is a wonderful expression of His power. We have access to that power by asking for His direction and then being obedient to His plan.

*A kinsman redeemer is a male relative who, according to various laws found in the Pentateuch, had the privilege or responsibility to act for a relative who was in trouble, danger, or need of vindication.

Live It Out

1. Explain how we can see God's power through His guidance and direction.

2. How did God show His power in Ruth's life?

3. Name a time when God directed you to a specific choice, decision, or action. Did you follow His guidance? What were the results?

Prayer Point

Write out a prayer praising God for His guidance in your life. Ask Him to point out any areas where you might not be following His direction.

Further Study

James 1:5
If you need wisdom, ask our generous God, and he will give it to you. He will not rebuke you for asking.

God will give us wisdom if we will only _____, and He will do it _____.

Psalm 5:8
Lead me in the right path, O LORD, or my enemies will conquer me. Make your way plain for me to follow.

If we seek His guidance, the Lord will lead us in the _____ _____ and protect us from our _____.

Psalm 86:11
Teach me your ways, O LORD, that I may live according to your truth! Grant me purity of heart, so that I may honor you.

If we seek God's guidance, we can live according to His _____, and this will lead to a pure _____.

Read the following scriptures and write out the key words and meaning of these verses.

Exodus 33:12-16

Job 6:24

Psalm 27:11

Psalm 31:3

Psalm 61:1-2

Psalm 143:8

Psalm 43:3

Psalm 16:7-8

Pearls of Wisdom/Notes

Moving On
In preparation for Lesson 5, read about Hannah in 1 Samuel, Chapters 1 and 2.

✝

And she made this vow: "O LORD of Heaven's Armies, if you will look upon my sorrow and answer my prayer and give me a son, then I will give him back to you. He will be yours for his entire lifetime, and as a sign that he has been dedicated to the LORD, his hair will never be cut."
1Samuel 1:11

Lesson 5

The Power of Prayer
Hannah

And she made this vow: "O LORD of Heaven's Armies, if you will look upon my sorrow and answer my prayer and give me a son, then I will give him back to you. He will be yours for his entire lifetime, and as a sign that he has been dedicated to the LORD, his hair will never be cut.
1 Samuel 1:11

Read 1 Samuel, Chapters 1 and 2.

God's power is revealed in His answer to our prayers!

Hannah was one of the two wives of Elkanah. Elkanah's other wife, Penin'nah, had sons and daughters. She constantly mocked Hannah because the Lord had not given Hannah children.

One day when Hannah could no longer bear the pain of her empty womb, she went to the temple to present her supplication to the Lord. She cried out to the Lord and wept bitterly. She prayed the prayer that we find in 1 Samuel 1:11.

After she said this prayer out loud she continued to pray silently, making a vow to God. Her lips were moving and the priest, Eli, accused her of being drunk. She explained to him that she was praying and had not had wine or drink. She told Eli that she was praying to the Lord. Eli prayed with her and told her to go in peace.

*As she was praying to the L*ORD*, Eli watched her. Seeing her lips moving but hearing no sound, he thought she had been drinking. "Must you come here drunk?" he demanded. "Throw away your wine!" "Oh no, sir!" she replied. "I haven't been drinking wine or anything stronger. But I am very discouraged, and I was pouring out my heart to the L*ORD*. Don't think I am a wicked woman! For I have been praying out of great anguish and sorrow."*
1 Samuel 1:12-16

Not long after her visit to the temple, she found out she was pregnant. When she delivered her son, she called him Samuel which means "asked of God". Hannah never forgot her promise to God. As soon as Samuel was weaned, she presented him to the Lord. When she arrived at the temple that same priest, Eli, was there. Hannah reminded him of the time that she prayed to the Lord for a son and then she dedicated Samuel to the Lord.

When the child was weaned, Hannah took him to the Tabernacle in Shiloh. They brought along a three-year-old bull for the sacrifice and a basket of flour and some wine. After sacrificing the bull, they brought the boy to Eli. "Sir, do you remember me?" Hannah asked. "I am the very woman who stood here several years ago praying to the Lord. I asked the Lord to give me this boy, and he has granted my request. Now I am giving him to the Lord, and he will belong to the Lord his whole life."
1 Samuel 1:24-28

Samuel was born as a result of his mother's prayer. Hannah yielded to God's power and trusted Him to fulfill her request.

I can't begin to count the number of prayers God has answered in my life. From physical protection to spiritual insight, God has answered prayer. The answers don't always appear in the manner that I expected but they are always perfect.

If we are to become women of power with God, we must develop a strong prayer life. It is such a privilege that we can seek the Lord in prayer. The Lord loves our prayers. He wants us to seek His guidance. He wants us to praise and worship Him.

God wants us to seek His power in our lives through prayer!

Live It Out

1. Hannah had good reason to be discouraged. What were her choices in this situation?

2. What commitment did Hannah make to God in her prayer? (1 Samuel 1:11) How did desperation change Hannah's prayer?

3. Have you ever made promises to God in your prayers? Did you follow through on those promises? Why or why not?

Prayer Point

Write out a prayer praising God for keeping His promises. Ask the Lord to help you operate in His power through prayer and meditation.

Further Study

Matthew 7:11
So if you sinful people know how to give good gifts to your children, how much more will your heavenly Father give good gifts to those who ask him.

God wants to give _____ _____ to those who _____.

1 Chronicles 16:11
Search for the L<small>ORD</small> and for his strength; continually seek him.

To operate in God's power, we must seek the Lord's_____ continually.

Philippians 4:6
Don't worry about anything; instead, pray about everything. Tell God what you need, and thank him for all he has done.

Paul's advice is to turn our _____ into _____.

Read the following scripture and write out the key words and meaning of these verses.

Luke 6:12

Psalm 4:1

Psalm 145:18

Proverbs 15:29

Luke 18:1

Romans 8:26

Colossians 4:2

1 Thessalonians 5:17

1 Timothy 2:8

Pearls of Wisdom/Notes

Moving On

In preparation for Lesson 6, read about Abigail in 1 Samuel 25 through 2 Samuel 2.

She fell at his feet and said, "I accept all blame in this matter, my lord. Please listen to what I have to say."
1 Samuel 25:24

Lesson 6

The Power of Humility
Abigail

She fell at his feet and said, "I accept all blame in this matter, my lord. Please listen to what I have to say."
1 Samuel 25:24

God's power is displayed in humility!

A humble position is a powerful position. As we become women of power in God, we must learn the importance of humility and then put that into practice.

We can learn a great deal about humility and the power of God through the story of Abigail, a humble, beautiful and intelligent woman. Abigail's husband, Nabal, was mean, spiteful and dishonest.

After the death of Samuel, David moved down to the wilderness of Maon. He became aware of Nabal who was shearing his sheep at the time. Nabal was very prosperous and owned three thousand sheep and a thousand goats. David sent word to Nabal asking for provision for his men who had protected Nabal's herds. Nabal rudely refused this request, going against the code of hospitality of the day.

Nabal was very rich and could have easily afforded to meet David's needs. It wasn't a handout request, but rather provision in exchange for protection. But Nabal's selfishness won out and he refused to assist the men. When David heard this, his mission was to seek vengeance against this selfish man.

"Get your swords!" was David's reply as he strapped on his own. Then 400 men started off with David, and 200 remained behind to guard their equipment. 1 Samuel 25:13

One of Nabal's servants relayed this situation to Abigail. He explained that David's men had actually protected them. Abigail realized that there would be trouble for her family if she did not intervene.

Abigail immediately gathered provisions for David's men and rode her donkey out to meet them. When Abigail saw David, she bowed low before him.

She fell at his feet and said, "I accept all blame in this matter, my lord. Please listen to what I have to say. I know Nabal is a wicked and ill-tempered man; please don't pay any attention to him. He is a fool, just as his name suggests. But I never even saw the young men you sent. 1 Samuel 25: 24-25

Abigail was humble and honoring to David, offering up the provision she brought for him and his men.

And here is a present that I, your servant, have brought to you and your young men. Please forgive me if I have offended you in any way. The L0RD will surely reward you with a lasting dynasty, for you are fighting the L0RD's battles. And you have not done wrong throughout your entire life. 1 Samuel 25:27-28

David was grateful and thanked God because her actions prevented him from carrying out his own vengeance against Nabal's family. He accepted her gifts and assured her he would not kill her husband.

Nabal was drunk when Abigail arrived home so she chose to wait to tell him what she had done. The next day, she explained that she had met with David and what had transpired. Upon hearing this, Nabal had a stroke and died about ten days later.

When David heard of Nabal's death, he immediately sent a message to Abigail asking her to marry him. Once again, Abigail displayed humility and honor to God in response to David's proposal.

She bowed low to the ground and responded, "I, your servant, would be happy to marry David. I would even be willing to become a slave, washing the feet of his servants!" 1 Samuel 25:41

God's power can work through us as we live as humble servants to Him!

Live It Out

1. How was God's power displayed through Abigail's humility?

2. It has been said that being humble is being weak. Do you agree? Why or why not?

3. What are 3 signs of humility?

Prayer Point

Write out a prayer asking God to help you live a humble life. Ask Him to point out any areas of your life where this is a challenge.

Further Study

2 Chronicles 7:14
Then if my people who are called by my name will humble themselves and pray and seek my face and turn from their wicked ways, I will hear from heaven and will forgive their sins and restore their land.

If we _____ ourselves and _____, God will _____ our land and _____ our sins.

Mark 10:45
For even the Son of Man came not to be served but to serve others and to give his life as a ransom for many."

Jesus came not to be served, but to _____.

Proverbs 11:2

Pride leads to disgrace, but with humility comes wisdom.

Humility brings _____.

Read the following scriptures and write out the key words and meaning of these verses.

Deuteronomy 8:2-3

2 Chronicles 7:14

Psalms 25:9

Psalms 55:19

1 Peter 5:5

Zechariah 9:9

Mark 10:45

Philippians 2:5-8

Genesis 18:27

Pearls of Wisdom/Notes

Moving On

In preparation for Lesson 7, please read the story of Deborah in Judges 4-5.

Deborah, the wife of Lappidoth, was a prophet who was judging Israel at that time. **Judges 4:4**

Lesson 7

The Power of Wisdom
Deborah

Deborah, the wife of Lappidoth, was a prophet who was judging Israel at that time. Judges 4:4

God's power is displayed through wisdom!

As women with a desire to operate in God's power, we must seek His wisdom.

Deborah was an exceptional woman. She was a female judge in Israel, with special abilities as a mediator, advisor and counselor. She was known for her prophetic power and wisdom. God trusted her to lead, and in His sovereignty and power, He raised her up as a judge in Israel.

Deborah wasn't anything like the female judges we see today on popular television shows! She wasn't harsh, condescending or vicious in her treatment of people. God's power worked through her in wisdom, courage and faith.

God called her a prophetess, meaning that she counseled with the Lord before she made any major decision. She operated in God's power through His prophetic guidance and wisdom. Judge Deborah was neither power hungry nor manipulative. She gave God the glory and credit in all situations.

Deborah was wise and also very courageous. Her courage was displayed when she summoned Barak:

One day she sent for Barak son of Abinoam, who lived in Kedesh in the land of Naphtali. She said to him, "This is what the LORD, the God of Israel, commands you: Call out 10,000 warriors from the tribes of Naphtali and Zebulun at Mount Tabor. And I will call out Sisera, commander of Jabin's army, along with his chariots and warriors, to the Kishon River. There I will give you victory over him. Judges 4: 6-7

Barak told her, "I will go, but only if you go with me." Judges 4:8

Deborah's response to Barak was that she would go with him, but by doing so, he would receive no honor or credit.

"Very well," she replied, "I will go with you. But you will receive no honor in this venture, for the LORD's victory over Sisera will be at the hands of a woman." So Deborah went with Barak to Kedesh. At Kedesh, Barak called together the tribes of Zebulun and Naphtali, and 10,000 warriors went up with him. Deborah also went with him. Judges 4:9-10

Deborah was responsible for leading the people into battle, but more than that, she influenced them to live for God. Her wisdom came directly from her faith in God and her willingness to allow Him to work through her.

In Chapter 5 of Judges, Deborah and Barak sang a song of praise and worship to the Lord. The song set to music the story of Israel's great victory. All glory and honor went to the One who deserved the credit.

God is our true source of wisdom.

We must plug into the power of God's wisdom by seeking Him out, listening to His wisdom and walking in it daily!

Live It Out

1. What were some ways that Deborah exhibited wisdom in Judges 4?

2. How do you think prophecy and wisdom are connected in the life of Deborah?

3. How can we plug into the power of God's wisdom?

Prayer Point

Write out a prayer praising and thanking God for His wisdom. Ask Him to show you ways to operate in the power of His wisdom at all times.

Further Study

Proverbs 9:9
Instruct the wise, and they will be even wiser. Teach the righteous, and they will learn even more.

Even those considered wise can be _____ _____.

Proverbs 13:14
The instruction of the wise is like a life-giving fountain; those who accept it avoid the snares of death.

Wisdom is like a life-giving _____.

Ephesians 5:15-16
So be careful how you live. Don't live like fools, but like those who are wise.

Write out the meaning of this verse in your own words.

Read the following scriptures and write out the key words and meaning of these verses.

Psalm 111:10

Job 12:12

Proverbs 3:7

Job 28:28

Proverbs 9:10

Ecclesiastes 7:12

James 1:5

Proverbs 14:8

James 3:17

Pearls of Wisdom/Notes

Moving On

In preparation for Lesson 8, read about Priscilla and Aquila in Acts 18; Romans 16:3-5; 1 Corinthians 16:19 and 2 Timothy 4:19.

Give my greetings to Priscilla and Aquila, my co-workers in the ministry of Christ Jesus. In fact, they once risked their lives for me. I am thankful to them, and so are all the Gentile churches. Romans 16:3-4

Lesson 8

The Power of Devotion
Priscilla and Aquila

Give my greetings to Priscilla and Aquila, my co-workers in the ministry of Christ Jesus. In fact, they once risked their lives for me. I am thankful to them, and so are all the Gentile churches. Romans 16:3-4

This lesson applies to all women, whether married or unmarried

Priscilla and Aquila…the ultimate power couple! They were devoted to the Lord, and to each other.

We hear a great deal about power couples today. Wealth, career, and influence earmark a power couple in our society. Priscilla and Aquila are powerful examples of the devotion we can develop when we plug into the power of God.

It is interesting that their names always appear together in the Bible, indicating a mighty unity and oneness. The first mention shows up in Acts 18:1-3:

Then Paul left Athens and went to Corinth. There he became acquainted with a Jew named Aquila, born in Pontus, who had recently arrived from Italy with his wife, Priscilla. They had left Italy when Claudius Caesar deported all Jews from Rome. Paul lived and worked with them, for they were tentmakers just as he was.

Priscilla and Aquila worked together, ministered together and learned God's word together. The source of power for these two came from God. He was at the center of every part of their life and marriage. This couple modeled devotion, equality and submission in their marriage. Devotion to the Lord first, then to each other.

Priscilla is the diminutive of Prisca, meaning "worthy". This name is also found as a family name in the earliest Roman annals, and appears in the form "Prisca" in Paul's Second Epistle to Timothy. It is also interesting to note that Aquila, Priscilla's husband, had the family name of the commander of a legion, for it means "eagle"— emblem of the Roman army. Both names are Roman. From the prominence given in Roman inscriptions and legends to the name Prisca it is concluded that she belonged to a distinguished Roman family.

Since the two are always named together, it is difficult to separate Priscilla out. Their two hearts beat as one; harmoniously, they worked together to serve the church. Both are mentioned six times and the name, Priscilla, comes first in three instances. They are never mentioned separately. It is interesting that Aquila is not named first every time, but shares mention with Priscilla. There are a few theories as to why this is so.

Dinsdale Young says "Priscilla may have been a believer before her husband, and that she won him for the Lord by her chaste conversation, or that perhaps hers was a primacy of character and service, or a more conspicuous intellectual ability, or that she may have been of nobler birth and social quality than Aquila."

Whatever the reason, it was highly unusual for her name to be mentioned before her husband's.

Priscilla was one with Aquila in marriage, with the Lord and in their secular business or "tent making". They are an early example of bi-vocational ministers (ministers with a secular job). They ran a home church together and taught (corrected) Apollos in Acts 18: 24-26:

Meanwhile, a Jew named Apollos, an eloquent speaker who knew the Scriptures well, had arrived in Ephesus from Alexandria in Egypt. He had been taught the way of the Lord, and he taught others about Jesus with an enthusiastic spirit and with accuracy. However, he knew only about John's baptism. When Priscilla and Aquila heard him preaching boldly in the synagogue, they took him aside and explained the way of God even more accurately.

The devotion exemplified in Priscilla's life is one we must take note of, as women. Married or not, our first priority is our relationship with God. Our devotion to Him comes first. If you are unmarried, prepare now by loving and being solely devoted to God as you wait for your husband. Married women, love the Lord and you will find being devoted to your husband easy.

Priscilla obviously operated in God's power in a way that most women did not in her day. She was plugged into the power of our great God!

Live It Out

1. What do you see that made Priscilla and Aquila a "power couple"?

2. What are some examples of her devotion to God and to her husband?

3. List 3 things you can do today to increase your devotion to God and your husband, if you are married.

4. What types of challenges might Priscilla have faced as a wife and a woman in ministry?

Prayer Point

Write out a prayer praising God for His presence in your life. Ask Him to help you understand the meaning of devotion to Him, and ways to deepen your relationship.

Further Study

*Honor the L*ORD *with your wealth and with the best part of everything you produce.* Proverbs 3:9

When are to honor the Lord with the _____ _____ of everything we have.

No one can serve two masters. For you will hate one and love the other; you will be devoted to one and despise the other. You cannot serve God and be enslaved to money. Luke 16:13

If we are devoted to God, we cannot be devoted to _____.

But don't just listen to God's word. You must do what it says. Otherwise, you are only fooling yourselves. James 1:22

If we are devoted to God, we will not just _____ to God's word, but we will ___ what the word says.

Read the following scriptures and write out the key words and meaning of these verses.

2 Timothy 3:16-17

Hebrews 13:5

Philippians 4:8-9

Colossians 3:1

Colossians 3:12-14

2 Timothy 2:15

James 1:19-20

Matthew 6:1

Acts 20:35

Pearls of Wisdom/Notes

Moving On
In preparation for Lesson 9, read about Sarai (Sarah) Genesis 11-25 and Hebrews 11:11-12.

✝

It was by faith that even Sarah was able to have a child, though she was barren and was too old. She believed that God would keep his promise. And so a whole nation came from this one man who was as good as dead—a nation with so many people that, like the stars in the sky and the sand on the seashore, there is no way to count them. **Hebrews 11:11-12**

Lesson 9

The Power of Faith
Sarah

It was by faith that even Sarah was able to have a child, though she was barren and was too old. She believed that God would keep his promise. And so a whole nation came from this one man who was as good as dead—a nation with so many people that, like the stars in the sky and the sand on the seashore, there is no way to count them.
Hebrews 11:11-12

Operating in God's power increases our faith!

There is probably nothing harder than waiting. One way we often cope with waiting, is to help God put His plan into action. Sarah definitely tried this approach. Since she was too old to give birth to a child, she assumed that God had a different plan. After all, God told her husband, Abram (Abraham), that he would have descendants that matched the number of stars in the sky.

Then the Lord took Abram outside and said to him, "Look up into the sky and count the stars if you can. That's how many descendants you will have!" Genesis 15:5

Our logic often takes over, and we attempt to complete God's promises in our own strength. Becoming a woman of power with God means we put all of our faith in Him by plugging into His power!

Sarah was a beautiful woman who wanted a child more than anything. She made mistakes, just like we all do. She stepped ahead of God and tried to handle His business in her own power, by foolishly sending her handmaiden, Hagar, to Abraham.

So Sarai said to Abram, "The Lord has prevented me from having children. Go and sleep with my servant. Perhaps I can have children through her." And Abram agreed with Sarai's proposal. So Sarai, Abram's wife, took Hagar the Egyptian servant and gave her to Abram as a wife. (This happened ten years after Abram had settled in the land of Canaan.) Genesis 16:2-3

This was not how God intended to give Abraham and Sarah an heir, but was a mistake from which they learned to more fully trust in God. Once Hagar had Ishmael, Abraham's first son, Hagar despised Sarah. In return, Sarah dealt harshly with her handmaiden.

Years passed. Ishmael grew and had a relationship with his father. And still Sarah remained childless. Finally, when Sarah was 90 years old, God again promised her a son.

Then one of them said, "I will return to you about this time next year, and your wife, Sarah, will have a son!" Sarah was listening to this conversation from the tent. Abraham and Sarah were both very old by this time, and Sarah was long past the age of having children. So she laughed silently to herself and said, "How could a worn-out woman like me enjoy such pleasure, especially when my master—my husband—is also so old? Genesis 18:10-12

In spite of the initial laugh, Sarah came to truly believe God could and would do what He said. Looking again at Hebrews 11:11-12, we see Sarah's faith and belief:

It was by faith that even Sarah was able to have a child, though she was barren and was too old. She believed that God would keep his promise. And so a whole nation came from this one man who was as good as dead—a nation with so many people that, like the stars in the sky and the sand on the seashore, there is no way to count them.

When Sarah allowed herself to plug into, and believe in God's power, her faith increased.

Live It Out

1. Why do you think Sarah took matters into her own hands regarding having a child?

2. Did Sarah show evidence of faith in God when she did not see the promise fulfilled immediately? Explain.

3. Have you ever tried to take over for God? What was the outcome?

Prayer Point

Write out a prayer thanking God for His promises. Ask Him to help you increase your faith as you wait.

Further Study

So faith comes from hearing, that is, hearing the Good News about Christ. Romans 10:17

Our _____ comes from hearing the _____ _____.

And it is impossible to please God without faith. Anyone who wants to come to him must believe that God exists and that he rewards those who sincerely seek him. Hebrews 11:6

We must have _____ and believe that God _____.

You can pray for anything, and if you have faith, you will receive it. Matthew 21:22

If we have _____ and _____, we will receive.

Read the following scriptures and write out the key words and meaning of these verses.

James 2:19

Mark 11:22-24

Ephesians 2:8-9

Luke 1:37

Hebrews 11:1

Ephesians 2:8

1 Corinthians 2:5

Proverbs 3:5-6

James 2:24

✜
Pearls of Wisdom/Notes

✜
Moving On
In preparation for Lesson 10, read 2 Timothy 1:3-7 (Lois and Eunice), Psalm 103:17, Proverbs 13:22, Romans 8:17.

I remember your genuine faith, for you share the faith that first filled your grandmother Lois and your mother, Eunice. And I know that same faith continues strong in you. **2 Timothy 1:5**

Lesson 10

The Power of Inheritance
Lois and Eunice

I remember your genuine faith, for you share the faith that first filled your grandmother Lois and your mother, Eunice. And I know that same faith continues strong in you.
2 Timothy 1:5

We can plug into God's power and pass it down to the next generation through spiritual inheritance!

Timothy's grandmother, Lois, was the first one in his family to believe in God, and she raised her daughter, Eunice, to have the same faith. Timothy probably spent time with his grandmother, but even if he didn't, his mother had her own faith in the Lord, which she obviously shared with him.

We know that God's word does not return void as told to us in the following verses:

It is the same with my word. I send it out, and it always produces fruit. It will accomplish all I want it to, and it will prosper everywhere I send it. Isaiah 59:11

But the love of the Lord remains forever with those who

fear him. His salvation extends to the children's children.
Psalm 103:17

Lois loved and obeyed God. The Lord worked the same miracle of faith in her daughter, Eunice, and in her grandson, Timothy. Timothy's faith is the reason that we have the letters the Apostle Paul wrote to him. Timothy's grandmother, Lois, left a spiritual inheritance for her family that has benefited countless generations after her.

God's power and promises are part of our spiritual inheritance.

Good people leave an inheritance to their grandchildren, but the sinner's wealth passes to the godly.
Proverbs 13:22

As we strive to become women of power with God, we have an important assignment. If we are mothers or grandmothers (biological or spiritual), we have children to teach. We have a responsibility to the next generation to leave them a spiritual inheritance. The identity and character of generations of people are shaped by this inheritance.

Physical training is good, but training for godliness is much better, promising benefits in this life and in the life to come. 1 Timothy 4:8

This inheritance will not happen by accident. It will require us to teach the word of God to our children and most of all, to live it out in front of them.

There is a saying that "more is caught than taught." The best way to teach is by example. Our character, choices, behaviors and habits will have a significant impact on those following us.

Live It Out

1. What is the inheritance that Lois passed on to Eunice, and Eunice to Timothy?

2. What does the phrase "more is caught than taught" mean to you?

3. List 3 ways we can pass on our spiritual inheritance to the next generation.

Prayer Point

Write out a prayer praising the Lord for His goodness. Ask Him to help you recognize ways to pass on your inheritance of faith.

Further Study

Direct your children onto the right path, and when they are older, they will not leave it. Proverbs 22:6

When we _____ our children the word of God, they will not _____ it.

And you must commit yourselves wholeheartedly to these commands that I am giving you today. Repeat them again and again to your children. Talk about them when you are at home and when you are on the road, when you are going to bed and when you are getting up. Deuteronomy 6:6-7

We must commit ourselves to God's word and _____ them to our _____ by our actions.

Always thanking the Father. He has enabled you to share in the inheritance that belongs to his people, who live in the light. Colossians 1:12

God has _____ us to share in the _____ that belongs to His people.

Read the following scriptures and write out the key words and meaning of these verses.

Ephesians 1:18

Romans 8:17

Psalm 16:6

Colossians 1:12

1 Peter 1:3-12

Galatians 4:1-7

Psalm 2:7-8

Acts 20:32

Titus 3:7

Pearls of Wisdom/Notes

Becoming a Woman of Power with God

Small Group Leader's Guide

1. Come to the study prepared. Ask God to help you understand and apply the lesson to your own life. This will enable you to share personal examples with your group.

2. Pray for the women in your group. In order for the lessons to impact the group members, Holy Spirit must be at work in their hearts and lives. Pray for your group members daily.

3. Begin and end on time. Women appreciate punctuality. Begin your meeting on time, from day one. Ending the group on time is just as important. Often the women attending your group will have children to pick up, or appointments scheduled afterwards.

4. Explain to the group that these studies are meant to be discussions not lectures. Encourage everyone to participate, but realize that some may be hesitant to speak during the first few sessions. Others may participate easily.

5. Try to affirm people's answers whenever possible. The women of your group may be reluctant to speak up at first. Letting them know that you appreciate their thoughts and insight will encourage them to participate. Simple words of affirmation such as, "That's a great insight," "Good response," "Excellent idea," or "I hadn't thought of that before" are enough to show people that you value their comments.

6. Don't be afraid of silence. Silence usually seems longer than it really is and often people need time to think about their answer or comment.

7. Resist the temptation to answer your own question. As a leader, you want to avoid doing most of the talking. You may need to rephrase the question or ask it again. The women of your group will want to hear what you have to say but avoid dominating the discussion.

8. Never reject an answer, even if you think it is wrong. When you reject people's answers, it is easy for them to feel rejected as well, and they may decide that it is too risky to give their opinion again. A better response would be to ask them, "Which verse led you to that conclusion?" Or let the group handle the problem by asking them what they think about the question.

9. Avoid wandering. If the discussion wanders off subject, gently bring the group back to the question or scripture being discussed. This is often a big concern with small groups so be firm but kind and bring the subject back to the study as quickly as possible.

10. Be aware of the pace. This is a 12 week study. While you won't want to rush your discussions, you will want to stay on task and schedule as much as possible. The goal is to read through the lesson and the questions at a comfortable pace so that you finish at the end of the allotted time. Some lessons will require more discussion time than others. In some situations, you may want to stop and pray for one of your members. Each group will be different.

Snacks/Coffee

The leader/host may want to furnish snacks, coffee or tea or the group may want to rotate bringing a light snack. Be sure to make it clear how that will work at the beginning of the study.

Snacks should be served when the leader thinks best. Some groups serve coffee and snacks on arrival and others serve after study is done. The length of your meeting time can also help determine when snacks are served.

Suggested Timeline

90 minute study-
Greet, pray, worship: 15 minutes
Study/Discussion: 45 minutes
Prayer, snack and chat, clean up: 30 minutes

60 minute study-
Greet and pray: 5 minutes
Study/Discussion: 45 minutes
Prayer, snack and chat, clean up: 10 minutes

Answer Key
Lesson 1
Live It Out

1. What is the difference between natural (worldly) power and the supernatural power of God?
Natural power: Physical strength, or controlling power through money, position.
God's power: Supernatural, freeing, all powerful.

2. God's power is one of freedom and release. What does that look like in our daily lives? Allowing God's power to work through us is letting go of the control and trusting His power in all things, and all situations. It is true freedom!

3. Matthew 19:26--*Jesus looked at them intently and said, "Humanly speaking, it is impossible. But with God everything is possible."* How easy or difficult is it for you to believe this verse? Give an example that these words are true from your own life.
(Give a personal example)

Further Study

Psalm 62:11
God has spoken plainly, and I have heard it many times: Power, O God, belongs to you;
Power belongs to God.

1 Corinthians 6:14

And God will raise us from the dead by his power, just as he raised our Lord from the dead.
The same power that raised Jesus from the dead will raise us from the dead.

Luke 11:20
But if I am casting out demons by the power of God, then the Kingdom of God has arrived among you.
The power of God can cast out _____.

Lesson 2
Live It Out

1. List 3 ways we can plug into God's power.
Prayer, seeking His presence, learning to hear God's voice.

2. How can you incorporate these into your daily life? (Give a personal example)

3. Fear and unbelief can cause interference when we are trying to plug into God's power. How? List some specific examples.
Fear and unbelief can paralyze our prayer life and block God's power.

4. *Your own ears will hear him. Right behind you a voice will say, "This is the way you should go," whether to the right or to the left.* Isaiah 30:21 Think of a time when God spoke to you about a decision, choice or direction you should take. (Give a personal example)

Further Study

Matthew 7:7
Keep on asking, and you will receive what you ask for. Keep on seeking, and you will find. Keep on knocking, and the door will be opened to you.
Jesus tells us to ask, seek and knock and He will give us what we need.

Matthew 21:22
You can pray for anything, and if you have faith, you will receive it.
If we have faith, we will receive what we ask.

Hebrews 11:1
Faith shows the reality of what we hope for; it is the evidence of things we cannot see.
Faith is what we hope for but cannot see.

Lesson 3
Live It Out

1. What is the general theme of the book of Esther?
God's timing is perfect, God is sovereign.

2. What were some of Esther's strengths and accomplishments? Courage, willing to act, concern for her people.

3. How did God's power manifest in Esther's life? His power gave her courage, willingness to die if needed (Esther 4:16)

4. Give an example of God's power and provision in your life. How important was the timing of the event or circumstance? (Give a personal example)

Further Study

Habakkuk 2:3
This vision is for a future time. It describes the end, and it will be fulfilled. If it seems slow in coming, wait patiently, for it will surely take place. It will not be delayed.
We are to wait patiently for God's timing is perfect.

Isaiah 40:31
*But those who trust in the L*ORD *will find new strength. They will soar high on wings like eagles. They will run and not grow weary. They will walk and not faint.*
If we trust in the Lord, we will find new strength.

Galatians 6:9
So let's not get tired of doing what is good. At just the right time we will reap a harvest of blessing if we don't give up.
We will reap a harvest at the perfect time.

Lesson 4
Live It Out

1. Explain how we can see God's power through His guidance and direction. His power shows through His guidance and direction by always leading us to the best plan, choice or decision.

2. How did God show His power in Ruth's life?
Ruth was loyal and followed Naomi and her plan, and was led to Boaz's fields.

3. Name a time when God directed you to a specific choice, decision, or action. Did you follow His guidance? What were the results? (Give a personal example)

Further Study

James 1:5
If you need wisdom, ask our generous God, and he will give it to you. He will not rebuke you for asking.
God will give us wisdom if we will only ask, and He will do it gladly, willingly.

Psalm 5:8
Lead me in the right path, O LORD, or my enemies will conquer me. Make your way plain for me to follow.
If we seek His guidance, the Lord will lead us in the right path and protect us from our enemies.

Psalm 86:11

Teach me your ways, O LORD, that I may live according to your truth! Grant me purity of heart, so that I may honor you.

If we seek God's guidance, we can live according to His truth, and this will lead to a pure heart.

**Lesson 5
Live It Out**

1. Hannah had good reason to be discouraged. What were her choices in this situation? She could allow her anguish and pain to cause her to give up, or she could trust God to answer her prayer.

2. What commitment did Hannah make to God in her prayer? (1 Samuel 1:11) How did desperation change Hannah's prayer? She promised to dedicate her child to the Lord. Her desperation and anguish prompted this promise.

3. Have you ever made promises to God in your prayers? Did you follow through on those promises?
(Give a personal example)

Further Study

Matthew 7:11
So if you sinful people know how to give good gifts to your children, how much more will your heavenly Father give good gifts to those who ask him.
God wants to give good gifts to those who ask.

1 Chronicles 16:11
Search for the LORD and for his strength; continually seek him.
To operate in God's power, we must seek the Lord's strength continually.

Philippians 4:6
Don't worry about anything; instead, pray about everything. Tell God what you need, and thank him for all he has done.
Paul's advice is to turn our need into prayer.

Lesson 6
Live It Out

1. How was God's power displayed through Abigail's humility? She was honoring, submissive to God and generous and humble to David.

2. It has been said that being humble is being weak. Do you agree? Why or why not? (Give your personal thoughts and opinions)

3. What are 3 signs of humility?
Submission, selflessness, grace/honor.

Further Study

2 Chronicles 7:14
Then if my people who are called by my name will humble themselves and pray and seek my face and turn from their wicked ways, I will hear from heaven and will forgive their sins and restore their land.
If we humble ourselves and pray, God will restore our land and forgive our sins.

Mark 10:45
For even the Son of Man came not to be served but to serve others and to give his life as a ransom for many.
Jesus came not to be served, but to serve.

Proverbs 11:2
Pride leads to disgrace, but with humility comes wisdom.
Humility brings wisdom.

Lesson 7
Live It Out

1. What were some ways that Deborah exhibited wisdom in Judges 4? Summoned Barak after receiving instruction from God, agrees to go to battle with Him but states that all Glory will go to God.

2. How do you think prophecy and wisdom are connected in the life of Deborah? Deborah sought God and He gave her prophetic instruction. She always acknowledged God for her wisdom.

3. How can we plug into the power of God's wisdom? Seek Him out through prayer, the study of His word and worship.

Further Study

Proverbs 9:9
Instruct the wise, and they will be even wiser. Teach the righteous, and they will learn even more.
Even those considered wise can be even wiser.

Proverbs 13:14
The instruction of the wise is like a life-giving fountain; those who accept it avoid the snares of death.
Wisdom is like a life-giving fountain.

Ephesians 5:15-16
So be careful how you live. Don't live like fools, but like those who are wise.
Write out the meaning of this verse in your own words.

Lesson 8
Live It Out

1. What do you see that made Priscilla and Aquila a "power couple"?
They were devoted to God and to one another. They worked together and ministered together.

2. What are some examples of Priscilla's devotion to God and to her husband? She worked alongside her husband in trade and ministry, always keeping God at the center.

3. List 3 things you can do today to increase your devotion to God and your husband, if you are married.

4. What type of challenges might Priscilla have faced as a wife and a woman in ministry? The status of women of the day probably brought many challenges in the area of power, authority and her position as a partner to her husband.

Further Study

Honor the LORD with your wealth and with the best part of everything you produce. Proverbs 3:9
We are to honor the Lord with the best part of everything we have.

No one can serve two masters. For you will hate one and love the other; you will be devoted to one and despise the other. You cannot serve God and be enslaved to money.
Luke 16:13
If we are devoted to God, we cannot be devoted to money.

But don't just listen to God's word. You must do what it says. Otherwise, you are only fooling yourselves.
James 1: 22
If we are devoted to God, we will not just listen to God's word, but we will do what the word says.

Lesson 9
Live It Out

1. Why do you think Sarah took matters into her own hands regarding having a child?
She lost faith that God would give her a child, and like many of us, decided to make it happen her way.

2. Did Sarah show evidence of faith in God when she did not see the promise fulfilled immediately? No, at that time she displayed impatience and even doubt and unbelief.

3. Have you ever tried to take over for God? What was the outcome? (Give a personal example)

Further Study

So faith comes from hearing, that is, hearing the Good News about Christ. Romans 10:17
Our faith comes from hearing the good news.
And it is impossible to please God without faith. Anyone who wants to come to him must believe that God exists and that he rewards those who sincerely seek him. Hebrews 11:6
We must have faith and believe that God exists.

You can pray for anything, and if you have faith, you will receive it. Matthew 21:22
If we have faith and pray, we will receive.

Lesson 10
Live It Out

1. What is the inheritance that Lois passed on to Eunice, and Eunice to Timothy? They passed on their faith and the knowledge of God.

2. What does the phrase "more is caught than taught" mean to you? (Give a personal response)

3. List 3 ways we can pass on our spiritual inheritance to the next generation.
Share our faith by teaching the Word, sharing testimony and living our faith out in front of the next generation.

Further Study

Direct your children onto the right path, and when they are older, they will not leave it. Proverbs 22:6 When we teach our children the word of God, they will not leave it.

And you must commit yourselves wholeheartedly to these commands that I am giving you today. Repeat them again and again to your children. Talk about them when you are at home and when you are on the road, when you are going to bed and when you are getting up.
Deuteronomy 6:6-7
We must commit ourselves to God's word and   teach them to our children by our actions.

Always thanking the Father. He has enabled you to share in the inheritance that belongs to his people, who live in the light. Colossians 1:12
God has enabled us to share in the inheritance that belongs to His people.

Also available:

Becoming a Woman of Character
(12 week Bible study for women)
www.sherrypoundstone.com

Notes

Notes

Notes

Notes

Printed in Great Britain
by Amazon